co-operative games

ACTIVITIES FOR A PEACEFUL WORLD

peace pledge union

RESOURCES **ONLINE**
for our other publications,
campaigns and much more
visit
www.ppu.org.uk
or
our education resources at
www.learnpeace.org.uk

Originally published as PEP Talk 7 1985
Revised edition 1990
Abridged second edition 1993
Reprinted 1995 1996 1997 1998 1999
This revised edition 2002

Published by the Peace Pledge Union
41b Brecknock Road London N7 0BT
020 7424 9444
info@ppu.org.uk
www.ppu.org.uk
www.learnpeace.org.uk
Typeset & design PPU

ISBN 0 902680 41 2

Published with support from the Peace Research and Education Trust

contents

introduction

' *Co-operative games are not just good fun, they are also of great educational value.'* This short statement offers us an explanation why an ever increasing number of teachers and parents are now interested in co-operative activities. They are proving to be effective means for encouraging and enhancing the development of skills much overlooked in traditional didactic education. Empathy, affirmation, toleration, confidence, enquiry and communication can all be fostered through participatory teaching methods which lay emphasis on co-operation rather than competition.

This pamphlet aims to provide both a practical resource for teachers and parents wishing to try out some co-operative activities, and an analysis of the educational value of such activities.

In the opening article, Clive Baulch draws our attention to the importance of games and play in children's development. He argues that as far as children are concerned, co-operative games are the norm. It is only the projection of adult neuroses onto children that turns games into competitive exercises, which require winners and losers. Both Mildred Masheder and Judith Holland appreciate the short-comings of competitive education, and Mildred suggests that education could be more effective if the balance between competition and co-operation were to be adjusted.

Whenever the direction of educational method and content veers from the three R's path, purist pedagogues have been quick to ask for educational rationale and justification. In an attempt to identify criteria of effectiveness Judith Holland imagines what her class would be like had co-operative learning styles been commonly practiced since the start of her pupils' education. She is able to see a classroom very different from the one she sees on a Monday morning.

To complement the theoretical analysis, we have included four co-operative games lesson plans. Each consists of a selection of tried and tested co-operative games, the combination of which makes each lesson plan suitable for immediate use with minimal alteration. Maggie Freake, an Infant School teacher from Ilford, Essex,used many of the games with her class in a regular special games session. She describes her experiences,her successes and her disappointments. This edition adds her subsequent research and reflections.

Finally, conscious of the need for aid in assessment, we have included a sample Evaluation Sheet taken from Terry Orlick's popular *The Co-operative Sports and Games Book*. This sheet can be used as a guide by co-operative games facilitators for obtaining input from the players about the games.

The future role of co-operative activities in education is yet to be fully appreciated. To date it is, as with all progressive curriculum development, only a handful of dedicated teachers who are willing to try out co-operative activities in the classroom. What future do they have for inclusion in the slower developing school timetable? Anthony Weaver suggested that *'the transformation of play into art could become the most potent and significant contribution of the present movement towards co-operative games. Many of them are already on the verge of dance and drama, painting and craft.*

'Dare we recognise, with acknowledgement to Jung and Herbert Read, that these four are the divisions into which the primary school curriculum naturally falls, but together they form a unity which is the unity of the harmoniously developing personality?'
Richard Yarwood

playing games

clive baulch

THE DIVISION between games and play is a purely artificial one devised by social scientists, educationalists, and child psychologists; adults all.

'He took up his brush and went tranquilly to work. Ben Rogers hove in sight presently – the very boy, of all boys, whose ridicule he had been dreading. Ben's gait was the hop-skip-and-jump – proof enough that his heart was light and his anticipation high. He was eating an apple, and giving a long, melodious whoop, at intervals, followed by a deep-toned dingdong-dong, ding-dong-dong, for he was personating a steamboat. As he drew near, he slackened speed, took the middle of the street, leaned far over to starboard and rounded to ponderously and with laborious pomp and circumstance – for he was personating the 'Big Missouri', and considered himself to be drawing nine feet of water. He was boat and captain and engine-bells combined, so he had to imagine himself standing on his own hurricane-deck giving the orders and executing them ...'(Tom Sawyer)

That description by Mark Twain, who was an avid observer of life, is a beautiful vignette of a child at play. Clearly, children play at games and for them there is no difference – games are play.

When adults play they do so primarily for recreation. It is this opposition to work which gives play a number of connotations. One of these is 'mere fun'. In puritan minds, however, mere fun is sinful; *'gather the flowers of pleasure in the fields of duty'* is an early Quaker saying. It is to this attitude, *'the protestant work ethic'*, so well written about by R H Tawney, that capitalism owes its success. Play is not work; it does not produce commodities in a marxist sense. Where it does, it 'goes professional' and ceases to be play. The professional game of soccer, which is a multi-million pound business, is, by this definition, not a game. This makes any comparison between adult's and child's play totally meaningless. The adult is a commodity-producing and commodity-exchanging being, whereas the child is only preparing to become one. An adult uses his or her recreation to step outside those defined limitations which are social reality.

For a child social reality is play, for through the playing of games a child learns to manipulate, control and master her or his world. A playing adult steps sidewards into another reality; the playing child advances forward into a new stage of being. Play, for a child, is not work, but neither is it recreation.

'It dawns on us, then, that the theories of play which are advanced in our culture and which take as their foundation the assumption that in children, too, play is defined by the fact that it is not work, are really only one of many prejudices by which we exclude our children from an early source of identity.' (Erikson, Early Childhood and Society, 1951.)

Adult play, or recreation, is supposedly fun, and yet the leisure and recreation that most adults indulge in is a multi-billion pound industry. Walk into any bookshop and see the volumes of books written about any of a dozen different sports/games/pastimes. Pick one up and you will discover one very clear message. If you are willing to work at it, you can be the best, you can be a winner. This inherent need to turn even play into competition is, unfortunately, an integral part of the capitalist economic system. Competition is the name of the game.

'Because our sports are so highly competitive, we may tend to believe that all human beings, especially males, are born competitors, driven by their genetic nature to the proposition that winning is 'the only thing'! The games of many cultures, however, have no competitive element whatsoever...Indeed, the notion that human evolve only through grinding competition with nature and each other is a false one. Charles Darwin is clear on the point that, for the human race, the highest survival value lies in intelligence, a moral sense, and social co-operation, not competition.' (George Leonard, The Ultimate Athlete, 1974.)

We might add, not only Darwin, but Leakey, Mead, and Montagu too, have argued against the theory that competitiveness is, in any sense, innate.

Co-operative games or play should not be seen as a contradiction in terms. On the contrary, as far as child play is concerned, they are the norm.

Iona and Peter Opie (**Children's Games in Street and Playground**, *1969*) found that when left to their own devices, unorganised by adults, the games that children played were, according to one's viewpoint, often extraordinarily naive or highly civilised. *'They seldom need an umpire, they rarely trouble to keep score, little significance is attached to who wins or who loses, they do not require the stimulation of prizes, it does not seem to worry them if a game is not finished.'*

Only adults worry about such things, but the tragedy is that they project their neurotic obsessions onto the children. This adults can do because the relationship between children and adults is an extremely unequal one. In our society adults have real powers (economic, social, legal, moral) over children, who have few rights, but a lot of obligations towards adults.

In 1974 *The New Games Foundation* was set up in the United States. It had a very simple brief: to spread the word about playing games 'just for the fun of it'. Pat Farrington, a community worker and founding member of *New Games*, had this to say about the underlying philosophy of the organisation: *'Games are not so much a way to compare our abilities as a way to celebrate them. I felt that by re-examining the basic idea of play, we could involve families, groups, and individuals in a joyous recreation experience that creates a sense of community and personal expression. People could centre on the joy of playing, co-operating, and trusting, rather than striving to win.'*

If you wish to create a play or any other type of community that will be strongly lasting, you cannot separate people into winners and losers. People must be encouraged to experience themselves as truly equal members. From its earliest days the *New Games Foundation* involved itself in community programmes. They used co-operative and trust games as tools for community building inside some of the toughest ghettos in the US and were very successful at it.

To truly understand co-operative games it is necessary that you play them as often as possible, because what these games are about is changing people's attitudes towards play and recreation. When you find yourself opposite someone, it is not because they are an opponent. When you are on a particular side it is not because that side is better than any other. You make the separation so that you can discover a new union. Co-operative games are challenging and they involve true, equal and just competition, but there is no value attached to winning. No-one keeps track of scores, no-one remembers who was last out – it doesn't matter. If there is no premium on being a winner, then no-one has to worry about being a loser. The only measure of success in co-operative play is whether everyone has fun playing.

If you have some spare time, spend it watching and listening to children at play.

You will develop a reverence for the games of children, for their ingenuity, for the subtleness of the rules, the encouragement of full participation, and the unimportance of competition. They are the complete opposite of those team games devised for them by adults. How we play games is much more important than we imagine, for it signifies nothing less than our way of being in the world. ■

the educational values of co-operative games

judith holland

WHEN WE advocate co-operative games and activities for children it is not just because they are good fun, although fun is one of the most valuable elements; rather, it is because the whole practice of co-operation is based on sound educational principles.

First and foremost is the ethos of the school and the home; if there is a spirit of co-operation in the air it provides the right atmosphere for learning, as well as for good personal relationships, and naturally the two are intrinsically linked. When teachers or parents co-operate with their children in play or some leisure activity, a wealth of good feeling is generated, which permeates their everyday lives. It is certain that we could all benefit, young and old, from a spell of co-operative games together, and the most prosaic of committees could make better decisions after a rollicking game of Musical Laps! The tension in a classroom can be greatly relieved by a game of Mushroom with a parachute in the playground or a Magic Circle activity indoors. At the seaside recently the relationships had become rather strained in the family I was with; then when we played a game of Join-hands-tag immediately the atmosphere was transformed into something joyful, not least because the young ones were able to feel that they were sharing mutual interests and were on an even keel with the adults. If we did manage to plan more time for this, the personal relationship between young children and adults would improve beyond all bounds.

In our schools the *hidden curriculum* is much more likely to promote an ethos of competition than one of co-operation, and there is a strong consensus of opinion amongst educators that this provides the necessary motivation for learning. At this point I would challenge the whole theory of motivation in education: very young children learn spontaneously, and it is only when we have thwarted their natural curiosity and interests by inappropriate and irrelevant learning that they resist and get into the carrot and stick relationship with their teachers. We should examine our whole approach to education, both teachers and parents, and scrutinise what children have to learn and whether the way of teaching it is active and experiential and whether they can relate it to their own experience and interests.

Let us be realistic about the role of competition in our educational system. As our present society is based on principles of the free market – each for self and the devil take the hindmost – it is to be expected that the spirit of competition should pervade all schooling and much of the expectations in the home. We cannot hope to change the basis of our educational ethos overnight and, indeed, many educators would urge for a balance between competition and co-operation, but at the moment the scales are heavily weighted on the side of a competitive, hierarchical approach. We need to enlist the support of the great educationalists of this century to explain why children's natural motivation is lost and why passivity and, therefore, boredom play an increasingly pervading role as the pupils attempt to climb up the educational ladder. Dewey, Piaget, Bruner, Donaldson and a host of others all agree that the learning process depends largely on the experience of the learner; passive rote-learning may give some immediate results, but real understanding comes with participation and action. This principle is well established in most nursery and infant schools in Britain today, but later on good practice is all too often thrown to the winds. There is no time any more for discussion and doing things together, everyone must get on. In following the guidelines and the philosophy of the educational theorist we could establish a better balance in our whole approach to learning, showing that not everything has to have a competitive element and that co-operation is the basis for good personal relationships, which should be a major aim in educating mature citizens of the future.

Of course, competition and co-operation are by no means always on the opposite sides of the spectrum; often they merge. Most team players have a deep sense of cooperating as a group. It may well be that spectators miss out on the intrinsically human aspects of group loyalty and are left with an imbalance of competitiveness leading to the crowd violence now so common at football matches. Group consciousness is an inherent human attribute, developing quite early in young children and well established by the age of seven and eight. As teachers, we should be able to channel this energy into the learning process, not by pitting one group against another, but by exploring the many ways in which co-operative skills can further their education. If we consider any activity we can perceive elements of competition and collaboration which can be drawn out, whether it is the way of examining the variables of a hypothesis or a simple game of Scrabble. There is also the concept of competing against oneself, which is as important for most athletes as the actual winning of the race; such attitudes promote supportive encouragement and could well play a much more extensive part in the classroom learning.

One of the areas of neglect in most schooling is the art of oral communication, with creative speaking and listening; this is specially true for the secondary school when teenagers need to express their ideas and feelings and try them out with their peers. This discussion process is fundamentally one of co-operation, although opinions may be highly controversial and heated, and if the habit is formed in early childhood it can pave the way for mutual understanding and tolerance in adult life. This applies equally to collaborative learning and peaceful conflict-solving, both in school and in the home. We are often led to believe that there are only two diametrically opposed solutions to any problem, and either you are on one side or the other. This dichotomy permeates much of educational practice: for example, the sciences versus the arts,

When I say co-operate, CO-OPERATE!

intelligence versus creativity, and especially in the realm of conflict-solving, violence or *laissez-faire*. Discussion techniques can help to clarify the other's point of view: there may be many possible solutions to a conflict and groups can pool their ideas and choose the most feasible. A good guide to such an approach is assertion training, where various solutions to a conflict situation are presented and the group has to decide what are *laissez-faire,* which aggressive and which assertive. This method could be used to advantage in the study of history, social sciences and current affairs. Apart from unfounded allegations of political indoctrination, this procedure can be assumed by harassed teachers to be time-wasting, particularly in view of the iron grip of the examination system; and so once more we miss out on the most valuable insurance against extremist viewpoints, that of pooling our ideas and sharing feelings. Again, this is not to deny a role for enlightened modes of assessment, but to make a strong plea for important aspects of human development, such as personal relationships and creativity, to be an integral part of the curriculum.

To give a specific example of this neglect, both in terms of creativity and the exploration of personal relationships, drama is non-existent in many schools and unimaginatively passive in many others. This is a co-operative activity *par excellence*, promoting a good self-image, which is the basis for good relations with other people; and whether it is spontaneous acting-out of difficult situations or combining for a finished production, the benefits are enormous.

Teachers who may begin with a few co-operative games in their classroom will find that there can be a new relationship between themselves and their pupils and this also goes for parents and their children. There are games that enhance the self-concept, encouraging choices so that all participants feel that they are special; trust games that inspire faith in their class-mates and their adult figures; co-operative games where no-one is the loser and no-one is left out; creative listening games – all giving a feeling of togetherness, which can enhance the life of the class and spread over the whole school. But this is only a beginning: the spirit of co-operation should act as a catalyst to encourage collaborative learning and to develop the skills of getting on with one's fellows and finally to emerge as an autonomous human being with the power to choose a future that will be life-enhancing and secure. ■

QUOTES AND NOTES

Dr Alice Miller:

All children are born to grow, to develop, to live, to love, and to articulate their needs and feelings for their self-protection.

For their development, children need the respect and protection of adults who take them seriously, love them, and honestly help them to become orientated in the world.

Children who are respected learn respect. Children who are cared for learn to care for those weaker than themselves. Children who are loved for what they are cannot learn intolerance. In an environment such as this they will develop their own ideals, which can be nothing other than humane, since they grow from the experience of love.

It requires no great effort to identify the apocalyptic features of our century: world wars, massacres, the enslavement of millions by technology and totalitarian regimes, the threat to the world's ecological balance, the depletion of energy sources, the increase in drug addiction. Yet the same century has brought us knowledge that is utterly new in human history: that the period of early childhood is of crucial importance for emotional development.

Ryelands County Primary School, Lancaster: 'Rights & Responsibilities' document:

The school is a fundamental and important part of the community. Schools and teachers have a duty of care, not only because it isn't possible to teach children who are experiencing serious social and emotional problems, but also because teachers and other educators, together with parents and other carers, have a moral obligation to inculcate future adults with ideals and a sense of fairness, co-operation and compassion.

This will not necessarily be in line with the present societal and establishment value system, which seems to be saying that competition is everything, greed is respectable, and care is of little worth because it isn't profitable. In this context some of the children may find it difficult to reconcile these conflicting ideas as they grow up. They may need a lot of help to understand why the school's expectations may differ from those that they encounter elsewhere.

co-operative learning

judith holland

TO LOOK into the future and try to visualise a schooling system where co-operative styles of learning have been adopted is an extremely difficult task. Since competition currently invades and pervades so much in education (and our culture) our very psyches are tuned in to only one way of operating.

'Compete with others. You are better, more competent, more aware, have more knowledge, have the right and, therefore, you may be the teacher and not the taught. Strive for a scale post and seek extra responsibility. Be the head and use your power and in the end you shouldn't worry about being an oppressor. Don't feel guilty – you have won in this game and we award winners with higher salaries and lots of status.'

Our minds so easily justify our positions of power because our competitive system fed and nurtured us on our inherent right to win.

It is inevitable that if some have the right to win, others will not have that same right and will have to lose. That's how competitive games go. Once you take up co-operative games where all are winners, the questioning of the game of life follows: you cannot think purely about children's play and how co-operative styles can be evaluated; you must also take up the larger issues of life.

Schooling currently alienates many,if not most,children. Carl Rogers (**Freedom to learn**, *Charles Maxwell, 1969*) has suggested that teaching in schools is built on a number of basic assumptions:

1. Pupils cannot be trusted to learn.
2. An ability to pass examinations is the best criterion for judging potential.

3. What a teacher teaches is what a pupil learns

4. Learning is the steady accumulation of facts and information.

5. An academic procedure, eg, the scientific method, is more important than the idea it is intended to investigate.

6. Pupils are best regarded as manipulative objects, not as persons.

Once we start to use co-operative learning techniques we shall be challenging these assumptions, and the learning process can become a natural and joyous thing.

There are several suitable manuals for teachers who want to develop co-operative games and work with a co-operative learning style. (See Resources.) All the handbooks include work in affirmation and peaceful conflict resolution. In many ways these are part of the style, rather than separate techniques. Affirmation work is quite difficult to begin with a class who are not used to it. In their last term at primary school I spent three mornings with around twenty children. I began each morning with a simple affirmation exercise.

The children found affirmation incredibly difficult. What were they were good at? Most of them were black, and from an inner city environment. They had already decided there wasn't much point in aspiring to achieve in a racist society. They seemed to know, at the age of eleven, that they were the powerless.

I would like to let my imagination wander and visualise that same junior class after eleven years of co-operative games and learning styles. If I can imagine eleven years with a different kind of education, I can see how I would develop criteria to judge the effectiveness of that style.

After eleven years of co-operative games and learning

▶ Listening is a very valued skill. The children have learned to listen to one another without interruption. They are able to maintain eye contact during their listening and it is a skill much valued in the classroom. Children use it to affirm others. 'I like Gavind, he is a good listener. '

▶ Imagination runs riot. Teachers have used books and followed ideas from manuals for games, exercises and co-operative learning techniques. By now, however, the children are inventing a handbook of the ones they like best. The book was produced co-operatively and everyone takes great pride in this achievement.

▶ The children have some set tasks, which they have agreed with the teacher are important for them to do. Other learning tasks are chosen by themselves. Small groups work together on their chosen topic. They use discussion, research, imagination, other people and, lastly, books to find out things they want to know. They present their work for evaluation by their classmates through spoken and written word.

▶ People are valued. Everyone tries to find out first if there is a person who knows an answer to problems according to who you are. They have learned how to make choices and feel satisfied with them.

▶ The children are very aware that there are forces at work in our world that separate people into the oppressed and the oppressor. They understand that sometimes they can be one and sometimes the other. They want to think about these things and try to do something to change. They have realised that similar forces operate in the classroom, and they have developed ways to arbitrate their own disputes. This is a clear sign that these children have used their skills well.

▶ In this classroom there is an adult who devotes much of her time to these children. Co-operative learning styles have taught her new ways. She is a good listener. She trusts the children to work and learn. She learns from them. Many other adults come into the room. They also work co-operatively and have built up resources together. They join in the sessions when everyone evaluates their work and sets themselves new priorities for the future.

My visualisation involves children of eleven. The nature of our primary education means it is quite realisable without too many fundamental changes in the system. Much more vexing is the post–eleven stage, where the whole system is geared to jumping through a hoop called examinations. I would welcome observations from secondary teachers who could extend this co-operative learning style and see how it would fit into this hoop. So many children leave school for the dole queues, where it does not matter how many examinations one passes. If children had worked co-operatively at problem solving throughout their secondary schooling, would they now be able to tackle the problems of unemployment together? Would those who do wish to pursue academic careers be able to take examinations when all their learning has been done co-operatively? How shall we evaluate good co-operators? As I reach the final paragraph, I realise I have uncovered more questions and revealed a woeful lack of answers. However, I am not depressed by this. Many of us on this path are dissatisfied with current straitjackets, and we shall search together for more healing and empowering ways of working with children and colleagues. Patrick Whitaker has a suggestion on how to begin:

'*The best way to begin is by regarding our classrooms as interactive work shops – places where learning and living are recognised as the same thing, where inner experiences are prized, where uncertainty is accepted and where mistakes are not necessarily things to be avoided. When thirty or so young learners are brought together with a skillful teacher, the potential for growth and development is enormous.*

We need to harness this potential which exists within each individual, as well as in the groups as a whole, by creating continual opportunities for reflecting on experience, becoming good at learning, and savouring the present reality of each pupil's life.' ■

co-operative squares

This game is played in groups of five. Each member of the group is handed a folder containing five pieces cut from five identical sheets of paper on which a geometrical shape, or any suitable black and white image covering most of the sheet, has been printed. The pieces have been jumbled, and the aim is to reassemble the five sheets correctly. This must be done in silence; each member of the group can only give a cut-out piece to the other members – none of the pieces can be taken. The game is over when each person has a completed sheet.

The details and structure of the game be varied in several ways, but the basic principle is the same: the aim can only be achieved through co-operation.

Pupils at Regents Park Girls' School, Southampton, tried this out. Some of them found it difficult not to hang possessively on to their pieces. 'You could see who likes to help others and who likes helping themselves.'

The liveliest part (not least because people could talk again) was the discussion afterwards, sharing the experiences of frustration and relief.

In fact, 'Squares' is not so much a game as a drama activity, its procedure followed by debriefing and analysis of what has been learned. Afterwards, groups can go on to devise improvisations of situations in which co-operation provides the most satisfying and satisfactory outcome.

The girls of Regents Park School worked together to devise other activities like this for their group to try.

Lesson Plans

Below are four popular lesson plans best suited to 6-11 year-olds, although the games have been played with success by older and younger children.

The games in each lesson are chosen to be compatible, starting with introductory games, building up to more energetic ones, and finishing with quieter, calming games; this is a recommended pattern, whatever the length of your session.

The plan assumes 45-60 minutes; judge by the degree of interest in deciding how often to repeat each activity. A few comments are added after each set of instructions to help give the essential feel of each game.

Lesson Plan A Indoors

A1. JUNGLE MORNING Everyone lies still on the floor. Imagine it is night in the jungle and all the animals are asleep. With the first light of dawn the animals stir, awaken, stretch themselves, yawn, begin to greet each other with their voices. The animals begin to move around, to touch each other, to speak by roaring, whistling, snorting, barking, etc., at each other – all the noise of a jungle waking up.
● *An introductory and energising game.*

A2. TOUCH BLUE Everyone finds a space and stands in it. The teacher says: 'Everyone touch blue' (or another colour). Players must touch that colour on another person. Endless variations are possible with this game, especially if you introduce objects and body parts, eg: touch elbow to another elbow.
● *An introductory game; very good for the less able-bodied.*

A3. MIRRORS Stand in a circle. Watch the leader. Leader moves very slowly using just hands, then other parts of the body and face. The others must move with the leader as if they were his/her reflection. The leader should stress the slowness and the togetherness of this game. Illustrate the difference between following and mirroring. Alternatively, the teacher could choose to do this as a paired exercise, in which case the pairs could take turns at being mirror and reflection, ie: leader and follower.

● *This game develops concentration, observation, group togetherness and silence. It is very good for drama warm-up and mime training.*

A4. LET'S BUILD A MACHINE Divide into groups of four–seven and ask groups to build a machine using themselves for all the parts. See that each person is completely involved, either as part of the machine, the operator or the product. Show the machine to the other groups. The leader/teacher could assign each group a specific machine. A variation might be to make a factory, using all the machines together.

● *A game for all abilities, developing inclusion and decision-making.*

A5. BUBBLES Everybody finds a partner and holds hands. Use all the space you can. Imagine you are bubbles floating in the sky, and walk very slowly and gently around the room. When you bump or brush gently against another couple your bubble pops and you swap partners. This is not a race.

● *A 'getting-to-know-you' game. If being used as an introduction game, encourage people to talk to each other as they walk around.*

A6. STICKY POPCORN Everyone finds a space and walks around the room with their arms outstretched. When you brush against someone else you stick together by holding hands, just like very sticky popcorn. Eventually, the whole class should get stuck together until you are all just one giant ball of sticky popcorn.

● *Another funny 'getting-to-know-you' game.*

A7. PASS THE SQUEEZE Sit in a circle. Link hands. One person (the teacher?) gently squeezes the hand of the person on the left or right. That person passes the squeeze on to the next person on the left or right, and so on around the circle and back to the leader. Some variations – the leader could pass a squeeze to the people on the left and right. Watch the funny confusion!

● *The first of a few sitting down games for catching breath and calming down.*

A8. DO YOU LOVE ME, HONEY? Sit in a circle. Starting with the person on the leader's left or right, the leader asks: 'Do you love me, honey?' That person responds: 'I love you honey, but I just can't smile.' The first person then attempts to make the second person smile. This can be by making a funny face or, perhaps telling a joke, or tickling. It is up to the leader to choose what will be allowed or disallowed in the round. This continues around the circle until the first person asked: 'Do you love me honey?' is made to smile.
● *Concentration, silence, fun, memory.*

A9. THROW THE MASK Sit in a circle. The teacher can choose someone to start, who has to make a mask of their face, as gruesome or as funny as they can make it. Then that person puts their hands up to their face, takes the mask and 'throws' it across the circle to someone else who catches it, puts it on their face and imitates it before wiping it off and making one of their own which they, in turn, must throw to someone else in the circle.
● *Observation and imitation. A good pre-drama warm-up game.*

A10. MAGIC MICROPHONE. All sit in a circle. An object such as a pen, shell, stone, etc. is passed from one person to another. Only if you have the object are you allowed to talk, otherwise you must stay silent. People must decide for themselves as to whether they wish to talk, or pass the object on without speaking. Can be used for co-operative story telling or for a class to tell the teacher their news, or to initiate a discussion where the teacher wants the shyer class members to participate.
/● *Concentration, listening skills, social development.*

A11. TROPICAL RAINSTORM Stand in a circle. One person acts as the conductor of the storm and starts off this symphony by rubbing her/his hands together, which the person next to them (choose which way you are going before you start) imitates, and then the next person and so on, until everyone is performing the same action. This is the increasingly heavy rainfall. The conductor then repeats the whole process with a new action – snapping fingers, hands slapping thighs, stamping feet – which makes the sound of the crescendo of the storm. As with any sudden storm, the conductor decreases the volume of the storm symphony by going through the above steps in reverse until the last person rubbing hands is silent.

● *A finishing game. Younger children are often awe-struck by this game's effects, and are left with a nice magic feeling. If there is stillness, allow a moment to enjoy it.*

LESSON PLAN B Outdoors

B1. NAME TRAIN Stand in a large, loose circle. One person is a railway engine and chuffs around the inside of the circle. The engine stops in front of a person and, if they know the name, shouts it out whilst simultaneously leaping up and down making semaphore movements. The occasional whoop-whoop of the engine whistle is also effective. The engine reverses and 'couples up' and then both engine and carriage go chuff-chuffing around the circle again until the engine stops in front of another person, when both engine and carriage shout out the name and make semaphore movements and whoop. Then the engine reverses and couples up again and goes around the circle until a name train composed of everyone is chuffing around the playground.

● *An energising affirmation name game.*

B2. HOW DO YOU DO Standing in a circle one person volunteers to be the host of this very funny party. The host walks around the outside of the circle and selects one player by tapping on the shoulder. The host shakes the hand of the guest and introduces themselves, saying: 'How do you do?' The guest answers: 'Fine, thank you' and says his/her name. They do this three times, and after the third time the host makes a dash around the circle in the original direction of travel, while the guest goes in the opposite direction. They are both trying to get back to the empty space, but when their paths cross they must stop and go through the entire ritual all over again and the guest becomes the host. You don't have to run, you can hop, or crawl.

● *An energising introductory name game, less suitable for younger children.*

B3. ELEPHANT AND PALM TREE Begin with everyone standing in a circle. One person stands in the middle and points to someone in the circle, saying elephant, or palmtree. To make an elephant, the person pointed to leans forward, clasping her/his hands and swinging arms to form a trunk. The person on the left makes the elephant's left ear by holding up the left elbow and touching the top of their head with their left hand. The person to the right of the elephant trunk does the same with their right arm to form the elephant's right ear. To make the palm tree, the person pointed to stands with arms straight up (the trunk). Those on each side hold up their outside arms, hands drooping, to make the fronds.

● *Fun and concentration.*

B4. FARMYARD The players stand in a large circle and choose a number of animals. For a group of twenty about six would be suitable. The names of the animals are written on pieces of paper, which are given to the players and should be as equally divided as possible. Then, with everyone's eyes closed, the players walk about and find their own kind by constantly calling out in the call of that animal – 'baa-baa', 'meow-meow', and so on. When two animals of one kind come across each other they should hold hands and find others of their own kind until the group is complete. The idea is not to finish first, but merely to find others of your own kind.

● *Introduction game. Trust game.*

B5. DRAGONS Get into teams of six to eight and find some space for each group. Each team lines-up and each person holds the waist of the person in front. These are the dragons-young and playful ones- and, just like puppies, they are always chasing their tail. The head of the dragon must try to tag the tail, but everyone in-between must prevent that from happening and protect the tail by jigging and twisting about. When the head has caught up with the tail perhaps they can change places.

● *An energising tag game. Great fun.*

B6. SAILORS The group forms a single file along a centre line. If the leader shouts 'Starboard', everyone runs to their right. If the leader shouts 'Port', everyone runs left. 'Shipshape' means back to the centre. Leader shouts commands faster and faster. See how confused people become.

● *Energising and warm-up exercise. Concentration.*

B7. ISLANDS Place several hoops (or sheets of newspaper) on the ground. Players swim walk round the room until a given signal, when everyone must stand on an island. Players move around once more and an island is removed. At the signal, once again, everyone must stand on an island.The game goes on, with an island taken away each time, until only one or two are left, depending on the size of the group. No-one must be left outside when the time for standing on an island comes. It can be done, if everyone helps.

● *Togetherness. Problem solving.*

B8. WIND IN THE WILLOWS The group forms circles of not more than eight people. One person stands in the middle of each circle with eyes closed. The circle stands shoulder to shoulder and faces the centre, hands held at chest height with palms forward. The centre person, who is the willow, stands with feet together and arms crossed over their chest. Keeping feet stationary and body straight but relaxed, the willow lets go and sways from side to side, forward and back. The circle, or breeze supports the willow with gentle pushes and makes summer breeze noises. Two people should support the willow at all times. Each can have a turn at being the willow swaying in the breeze.

● *This is a gentle trust-game suitable for older children.*

B9. CARWASH Form the group into two lines facing each other. Each facing pair become a different part of a carwash machine and makes the appropriate actions. Stroke,brush and gently pat as each car is sent through to join the end of this machine until everyone has been washed.

● *An affirmation,trust and quietening-down game.*

B10. MY BONNIE LIES OVER THE OCEAN Stand in a circle. Everyone sings 'My Bonnie lies over the ocean', until people are familiar with the song. Then sing the song again, but this time everyone moves their hands to show the waves of the sea. As the song starts hands go down gently until the letter 'B' is heard, then they rise gradually head high till the next 'B'. To reach the third 'B' hands sink smoothly deeper. For the chorus there are smaller waves, as the 'B's are closer. To make it more like the sea, whole body movements can then be used, bending knees to sink down, then standing tall to the crest of the wave. The last time through the song start some down hollows in the waves, and others high, the wave-tops.

● *Combining singing with sea movements concentrating to keep it going effectively. Tell players briefly about Flora MacDonald and Bonnie Prince Charlie, perhaps, share any experience on the sea. Aim for quiet singing and flowing movements. Those who don't know the song or don't wish to sing might be waves in the centre of a circle of singers.*

LESSON PLAN C Indoors

C1. JUMP-IN EXERCISE Stand in a large circle. One person jumps into the centre of the circle in a way that expresses how they are feeling at that time. Everyone in the circle has a go.
- *Warm-up game, good for expression of feelings, especially with younger age group.*

C2. KNOTS Everyone stands in a circle, shoulder to shoulder with closed eyes. Hold arms outstretched and move forward together towards the middle and wave arms around to shuffle them. Take another person's hand in your own and, when each person has two hands, then open eyes. Now, without dropping hands, try to untangle yourselves. The group works together to try and untangle the knot.
- *Group problem- solving , fun. May not appeal to children under seven.*

C3. PRETZEL Group holds hands in a line,except for two who stay out. The leader leads the group by hand and twists and weaves under and through the group without dropping hands, until the group is all tangled together. The two people (chief untanglers), advise the group how they can unknot themselves.
- *Decision-making (for the two), listening, togetherness,fun.*

C4. YES – NO Everyone chooses a partner and sits back to back. Everyone chooses whether to be Yes or No. Yes must try to push No across the floor while shouting: 'Yes, yes, yes', while No must try to push Yes across the floor while shouting: 'No, no, no' all the time. After a while partners may swap roles.
- *A good game for relieving frustration. Therapy. Fun.*

C5. ROWING BOAT Make teams of six to eight and sit on the floor one behind the other. The person at the front must pretend to row, and everyone in the boat must try to pick up the stroke or rhythm. When the stroke has been together three times then the person at the back is allowed to go to the front, and the whole process starts again. See how quickly you can progress up the river (room).

● *Group awareness and synchronisation.*

C6. CONTROL TOWER Everyone chooses a partner. The pairs choose who is to be the aeroplane and who the control tower. Make a runway of two rows of chairs and place obstacles along its route. The plane is blindfolded and the control tower must verbally guide it along the runway and round the obstacles for a safe landing. If successful, or if the plane crashes, the roles are reversed.

● *Instructions, listening. Success builds trust.*

C7. ZOOM Sit in a large circle. Imagine zoom as the sound of a racing car. Start by saying zoom and turning your head either to left or right of the circle. The person on that side passes the word zoom to the next person, and so on until everyone has passed the word zoom around the circle. If you wish to change direction, then you say the word 'eek' like the screech of car brakes. Zoom takes you off again after 'eek' in the opposite direction. It is probably best if you restrict the word 'eek' to one use per player.

● *Co-ordination for the younger child. Fun to speed up.*

C8. MAGIC WINKS Sit in a circle and pass a card to each player, who looks at it, and keeps it hidden. 'Ace of Hearts' is the magician, but no-one else knows this. The magician tries to wink at random individuals around the circle without the rest noticing. If you are winked at, you must leap up and freeze – the magician has hexed you. You can say nothing. People can try to guess who the magician is, but if they get it wrong they get 'hexed' too. Guess correctly and the magician loses power and everyone is unfrozen.

● *Concentration, eye contact, fun, social interaction, drama warm-up.*

C9. SQUEEZE AND STRETCH Each person sits on the floor in their own space. The leader talks the group slowly through the following sequence: sit in a hunched position, knees drawn up, arms clasped tight around the legs, head buried in knees, back arched tightly; calves, thighs, buttocks, neck, fists, feet – all clenched, every muscle tensed. Hold that position for five seconds, and then very slowly release and unwind until your body is really spread and relaxed. Then progress on to a stretching position when toes and fingers are spread, back arched and arms extended fully, all joints are pulled apart; face is opened with wide eyes, tongue out, etc. Finally relax fully.

● *Sensory awareness, body control, tension-release, relaxation. Mime and drama warm-up exercise.*

C10. HERMAN – HENRIETTA Herman-Henrietta is an imaginary blob of clay that can be made into anything. Sit in a circle. The teacher beginning to mime, pulls the imaginary blob of clay from her/his pocket and creates something with it, perhaps something easy to begin with. It is fun to guess what the object is, but not important as the object of the game is a quiet concentration on what another person is doing. After the leader has finished, the magical lump is pressed down to its original shape and passed reverently to the next person. The game continues around the circle.

● *Observation, concentration, basic mime.*

C11. LAPSIT Players stand in a circle, close together, all facing in one direction, each with hands firmly on the hips of the player ahead. Now walk very slowly forward and, on a given signal, everyone gently sits on the lap of the player behind. If players are co-operating, the circle will stay up and everyone will have a comfortable lap to sit on. If people do not sit gently or help others to find a seat, then the circle will fall down.

● *Group awareness. The game works best with ten or more people of the same size.*

Lesson Plan D Outdoors

D1. THE NAME OF THE GAME Stand in a circle. Someone throws an object to someone else in the circle while saying their own name. The recipient then throws the object to someone else in the circle while saying their own name, and so on around the circle. A variant for this game is to say the name of the person to whom you are throwing.

● *An introductory name game.*

D2. TOUCHBEE Stand in a large and loose circle. Someone throws a ball (or beanbag) to someone else in the circle. Everybody else walks/runs/hops across the circle, touches that person, says their name and returns. The touched person then throws the ball to someone different, who gets touched in turn, and so on around the circle.

● *A nice introductory affirmation game suitable for disabled people.*

D3. SCARECROW TAG Choose someone to be the leader/scarecrow. If a big group, ie over 20, choose two. The group must run from one straight line to another opposite, but if caught by the scarecrow must stand with legs and arms outstretched. They can be freed if someone crawls between their legs or ducks under their arm, but watch out for the leader scarecrow!

● *A co-operative tag game. Change the leaders frequently if playing a long game, as it is mighty tiring otherwise!*

D4. TRIANGLE TAG Divide the group into sets of four. Three of each set hold hands and form a triangle, and one of the three volunteers to be the target. The fourth person stays outside the triangle as chaser. The chaser tries to tag the target by touching an upper arm, but the three players forming the triangle co-operate to prevent that happening, protecting the target by jigging, dodging and moving about. The target cannot be tagged from across the triangle.

● *A co-operative (Euclidian!) tag game. Guaranteed to exhaust.*

D5. MUSHROOM All players stand outside the edge of the parachute canopy/sheet, crouch˜down and take the edge in both hands. People at random call out the names of their favourite fruit/vegetable and when the word mushroom is heard everyone must lift the canopy as high as they can. With younger children it might be best to go around the circle individually. For children who like to go under the canopy, one variation is, while the canopy is in the air, to call out the name of a colour, and persons wearing that colour can let go and run under the canopy to a holding space on the other side.

● *A good introductory game.*

D6. TENTS Start as Mushroom, but when the canopy is above the players' heads they should lift it behind them, bring it down and all sit on the edge. Choose one person to act as the tentpole and remember to have a lookout on the outside.

● *Another basic parachute game. Once inside the tent, you can play games such as C10 Herman-Henrietta, A7 Pass the Squeeze or A10 Magic Microphone.*

D7. ALLIGATORS Players sit around the edge of the canopy with their feet under it. Someone can volunteer to be the alligator, which crawls under the canopy. The rest of the players make wave effects on the canopy by shaking it as the alligator swims around the swamp. When the alligator touches a player's foot then that player has been eaten and turns into another alligator, who in turn must go and catch another player. This game usually ends in hysterical chaos with everyone under the canopy. So, for safety, allocate a lookout before you start.
● *Trust and some dexterity with the parachute.*

D8. CAT AND MOUSE Select a player to be the cat and another to be the mouse. The cat stands on the canopy and the rest of the players lift the edge of the canopy to chest height and start making ripples in it. The mouse goes under the edge of the canopy and runs around, making 'squeek-squeek' noises so as not to make it too difficult for the cat, who has to try and catch the mouse by touching its shape through the canopy. A very tiring game! Change mice and cats frequently to give everyone the experience.
● *A good exploration of the properties of the parachute.*

D9. FRUIT BOWL The group lifts the canopy up to chest height. The teacher selects one or two people (three or four if young and small) and asks them to stand in the middle of the bowl. The teacher throws a large ball into the bowl and the team in the middle have to throw the ball out again, while the rest of the group have to stop them. The group must not take their hands off the canopy, nor must they kick the ball.
● *Co-operation in handling the parachute.*

D10. PRU-EE The leader whispers in someone's ear: 'You're the PRU-EE'. Now everyone, including the Pru-ee, with eyes shut begins to mingle . Each person is to find another person's hand, shake it and ask 'Pru-ee?'. If the other person also asks 'Pru-ee?' they drop hands and go on to someone else. Everyone goes around asking except, the Pru-ee, who remains silent the whole time. When there is no response to the question 'Pru-ee?', the Pru-ee is found and the searcher hangs on to that hand, becoming part of the Pru-ee and also remaining silent. Anyone else shaking hands with the Pru-ee (now two people) becomes part of it, making it larger and larger. If someone finds only clasped hands and silence, he or she can join the line at that point. Soon the cries of 'Pru-ee?' will dwindle, and the Pru-ee will increase until everyone is holding hands. End of game.

/● *A good game to begin quietening down after a lot of physical activity.*

D11. RHYTHM CLAP Everyone sits in a circle and closes their eyes. Each player begins to clap or beat any rhythm he or she chooses. At first it will sound chaotic, but gradually people will find themselves doing remarkably similar rhythms.

● *Can be used by leader to slow things down. People who believe themselves to be without rhythm will feel very pleased with the activity.*

D12. PASS THE HUG Everyone stands in a circle. One person starts by giving a hug to the child on her/his left and so on around the circle.

● *A closing game.*

PARACHUTE GAMES

A comprehensive collection of co operative games played with a parachute for children and adults of all ages and abilities. £4.99 plus £1.90 p&p

Available from the Peace Pledge Union 41b Brecknock Road London N7 0BT. Tel 020 7424 9444, email info@ppu.org.uk

a teacher's experience

maggie freake

AFTER A few try-outs with my class (vertically grouped infants ranging from 4 – 8 years) during the summer term, I decided that co-operative games deserved the priority of a regular weekly time-slot for the school year. Otherwise, they would inevitably get crowded out by pressure from the myriad of other activities that go on in the infant classroom. So, regularly every Wednesday afternoon for an hour or more, depending on our mood and interest, we played 'special games'. This is not to say that the games existed in isolation. Their effect spilled over, and was particularly noticeable at times when the class gathered to talk as a group, and during PE lessons.

I tried out 25 or so games during the autumn term – from various sources. I had a lot of help from Clive Baulch who often assisted me at these Wednesday sessions, bringing moral support and extra goodies like the parachute, as well as a wealth of ideas for games. Of all the games we tried out, only three didn't work with my class! Over the next two terms I developed and added to the list, exploring lots of new games. Often I just adapted ideas from games I already knew. The games changed and evolved according to the children's reactions and ideas as we played them. With our aims of co-operation and enjoyment, this process happened spontaneously and easily and seemed to breathe life into the games. With time, the sessions became progressively easier and more relaxed.

the successes

The children first became noticeably enthusiastic about half-way through the first term when we played Sticky Sticky Glue with them. After that they would ask: 'Is Clive coming today?' As Christmas approached I realised that here was a golden opportunity to use co-operative games in place of some of the traditional competitive ones, and to introduce them to some new children. At Christmas our class doubles up for party games, so half the children in the class would know nothing about co-operative games. I discussed it with their teacher. I thought Touch Blue would be very good for nervy children, who worry if they are going to behave right at parties, not being quite sure what is expected of them (see *Lesson Plan 1, Game 2*). The physical contact is reassuring and makes everyone part of the group. Zoom, an early favourite of my class, was also good for including everyone in and making every child feel needed (*see Lesson Plan 3, Game 7*).

On Party Day these two games worked beautifully. They broke the ice and made the children feel relaxed and interested. Jigsaws (old Christmas cards cut irregularly into 4 pieces) was also a good party number. A child who can't understand the instructions and just stands by, clutching a piece of the puzzle, will soon be rescued by a quicker-thinking child because s/he needs that piece to finish the puzzle. No losers. No wall-flowers left feeling unwanted or inadequate. The atmosphere at the party was calmer and friendlier than usual.

I played the Other Lands game with the children because I was curious as to their reaction, but I did not expect anything like the interest it aroused. The story scenario is essentially this: on the way to 'nice land' your aeroplane runs out of fuel and is forced to crash-land in a country which is 'not nice'. We sat in a circle and I asked each question to each child in turn, so that each question was one round of the circle. The questions were:

'What is the place like?'

'You go to school there, what happens?'

'Perhaps the name of the country is … ?'

Answers got more imaginative as the particular questions went round. Different children's lands were different, but very related. They were listening to each other and drawing and building on each other's ideas in a very creative way. A lot of the children's answers were personally relevant and very real. A complete contrast to the original free-choice story-telling session we had tried in the autumn (which was an out-and-out flop).

Two PE sessions – one using just bean-bags, and one just hoops – were particularly successful when I structured them co-operatively. The most memorable bean-bag game was when I asked the children to transport the bean-bag with two children touching it in the most imaginative way possible. Usha and Noreen stood face-to-face with their bean-bag between their eyes, like a double blindfold, clasped each other around the shoulders and moved. They could not, of course, see where they were going! Everyone had to try that one. One of the hoop games was to get inside a hoop with your friend. I did not need to suggest movements – they just happened. Some hoops gyrated madly all around the playground; others went along rather like a horse and cart; some like a tandem. Musical hoops, a sort of co-operative opposite of musical chairs, was also good fun. As hoops are withdrawn the problem is not how to elbow another player out of the way, rather how to keep the player inside the hoop without the whole lot of you overbalancing. Our hoops became islands in a shark infested sea. The children found that a group cuddle was the only way to stay alive! And for once they didn't seem to notice that they were cuddling the opposite sex.

I think that one game in particular has had a very noticeable effect on the class – Magic Shell. We sit in a circle and only the child holding the shell may speak. The shell is passed around the circle until everyone has held it. I particularly like the way a more reticent child may hold the shell silently but thoughtfully before deciding not to speak this time and pass it on. I like the way it gives each child time and space to collect their thoughts before speaking, and I like the calm and respect with which the children have learned to listen to each other. This game has had a great influence on the form of our class discussions.

After a term of co-operative games, the children formed easily and spontaneously into groups at PE. Making a class line for a train, or a dragon, or a class circle became easier than it had even been. It was as though they were choosing to act as a group rather than individuals. Some kind of group bonding was taking place.

the disadvantages

Inevitably a more cramped timetable for all the other things that need doing during the week. But this happens with everything that is worth doing!

The main problem that co-operative games has thrown up is the polarising of children into single-sex groups during small-group games. The fear and stigmatising of the opposite sex becomes particularly visible. Firstly, as a feminist, I have to deal with my own anger at the society that conditions its children to believe that the touch of the opposite sex is in some way damaging. Then I have to deal with the situation – to find ways to counteract this conditioning. It remains an unsolved, but not, I hope, insoluble problem.

the effectiveness

The games give my class a good feeling of fun and togetherness, and they pull in children who might otherwise remain on the outside. (Last year my class had more than its share of children with problems – emotional, social, language, slow development.) Some children would opt out now and then and sit and watch, but usually they would want to join in the next game.

Co-operative games teach social skills in the best way by encouraging the children to be sociable and to feel good in the company of others. Failure has no place in these games. They treat the players kindly, and the ripples from this spread in all sorts of little ways: ripples of friendliness and humanity.

They make me as a teacher more conscious of each child as an individual personality, not just a brain. I am trying to motivate for success at the three Rs. Perhaps it is more important to focus on the four Cs – Confidence, Concentration, Communication and Co-operation. The three Rs offer too restricted a view of what schools should be about in this day and age. Through co-operative games the child is encouraged to develop as a whole person, and that to me is what education should be about. ■

Published by the Peace Pledge Union ISBN 0 902680 44 7

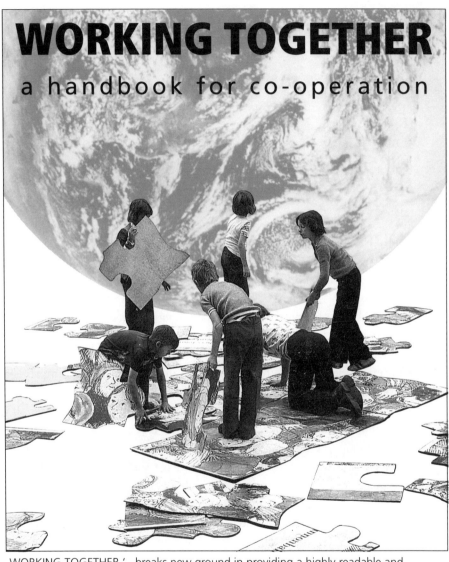

WORKING TOGETHER

a handbook for co-operation

WORKING TOGETHER '...breaks new ground in providing a highly readable and accessible introduction to co-operative skills.' Designed for parents and anyone who works with the young and is interested in promoting a war-free world. Price £10.50

PPU ACTIVITIES FOR A PEACEFUL WORLD

why use
co-operative games
maggie freake

THE MULTI-CULTURAL CLASSROOM

Co-operative Games are of great value in the multicultural classroom, like mine, where children do not all share a common first language, or culture. They 'include everyone in' and help us to enjoy playing together, thus strengthening the group bond, which bridges the barriers of language and culture. Although they have a common bonding effect, they aim, not at conformity or uniformity, but at a celebration of the richness of diversity of us as individuals and of our own uniqueness. So, being different from the norm is not something to feel ashamed of. This helps bilingual children to feel more valued.

As well as making the classroom a more relaxed and friendly place, which is a priority in itself, it will also make learning a second language easier for bilingual children. According to Cummins:'The motivation of children to learn L2 is closely tied to their attitudes to L2 speakers.' Or, in other words, the more they like the children who speak English, the more the bilingual children will want to learn English themselves. Skutnabb-Kangas makes a similar point: children with low anxiety levels and high motivation and self-confidence have less of an 'affective filter', ie, their intake tends to be higher for a given input of language. And again, Dulay, Burt and Krashen say, 'relaxed and confident students can learn more in shorter periods of time'. Not surprisingly, I have found the most noticeable effect is on the Stage 1 learners. The games offer them a way to communicate without language. They feel part of the class in a way which is impossible with normal language-based activities, especially if they are going through the silent period.

The feelings of belonging and acceptance that Co-operative Games engender are good for countering racism and sexism. Because the children enjoy the games, they will sometimes work with children they normally avoid, perhaps without realising it, and thus begin to relate to them.

Rejection is often closely bound up with taboos about touching. The Opies noticed a fear of touching particular children in their observation of playground games, and before I started Co-operative Games in my class, I had noticed particular boys who would not touch girls. In this kind of situation, it is ethnic minority girls who tend to suffer most, under the combined effects of racism and sexism. As we have played the games, the situation appears to have improved in my class, and children feel much more comfortable about touching each other.

Orlick says that the Co-operative Games created for his book evolved from his work and play with people all over the world, so they are essentially multi-cultural. He also points out that genuine Co-operative Games are extremely rare in the present day Western World, although they have been played in many other cultures for centuries. Games which accept and involve all the players and get them working together towards an enriching experience must needs be anti-racist. Many of the games value individuality by calling for personal creative actions as well – they do not treat everyone the same, but celebrate our differences. Because of this, I think they are inherently anti-ageist and anti-sexist as well. They are pro-people.

Orlick also mentions some games which are so co-operative and concerned for the other players' feelings, that the object is not to win but to tie. He cites Take-tak, a game which he says is popular among the Tangu people of New Guinea, because the dominant theme in their native culture is moral equality. Tying in these games, he says, requires a refined skill, both to hit taketaks (coconut spines) with the hollow seedpods, and also to miss them when expedient. Also, another New Guinea tribe, the Asmats, used to race dug-out canoes across a river, but 'always reached the other side at the same instant', and similar activities are to be found among the Eskimos and Aborigines. Tying could possibly require more skill than winning, which is a surprising thought, in direct challenge to my own westernised values. Orlick describes his own efforts at tying in a running race. It calls for immense control.

Both our society and our schools are run on very competitive lines. Davison says: 'Younger children are willing to compete, but after experience has shown them that rewards go continually to a few of the most adept, most children cease to try in the area where they can't win.'

THE WINNERS

Davison goes on to say that competition does help the better performers to learn, but they will then need 'evidence of superiority to sustain their self-respect'. In other words, if we motivate too much by competition, winners will become hooked on success, which is a very distorting influence. It teaches the winners:

1. To work harder in areas where they can excel, but also not to participate in those areas where they can't win.

2. Not to work when there is no reward (even if they want to work; it's better to save their efforts for when a prize is available.

3. To delight in others' failure. And as Terry Orlick says: 'They hope for it.. they help it happen because it enhances their own chances of victory.'

She goes on to say: 'Many children's games and programmes are, in fact, designed for elimination. Many ensure that one wins and everyone else loses, leaving sports 'rejects and drop-outs' to form the vast majority of our North American population.'

I myself watched a baseball game played in a park in Minnesota 18 months ago, and was horrified at the virulent put-downs issued by young men to members of their own team who didn't play perfectly. They seemed to be playing against their own team-mates, as well as the opposing team. This was no friendly game, full of team spirit.

THE LOSERS

And what does too much competitiveness do for the losers? It teaches them:

1. Not to try. Then you can't lose and you can't fail.

2. By giving children a negative self-image, it is also likely to encourage them to be anti-social and destructive, or as Davison says: 'to be good at "bad" things"'.

On an emotional level winners feel good about winning, but losers can feel angry, bitterly disappointed and devalued. It is as though the winners are feeding emotionally off the losers in a kind of parasitic relationship. I am not arguing that there should be no competitiveness. There can be elements of competition in some co-operative games, and team games can be a good mixture of competition and co-operation. A losing team who have played well together need not feel they are failures. Jim Wingate says: 'Removing the value judgement or labelling [of success/failure] from competitive activities moves them firmly towards being co-operative.' In other words, take the emphasis off playing to win, and put the emphasis on taking part.

Instead of an art competition, says Davison, hold an art display. Instead of the central position being given to the exhibits which win the prizes, it could be given to a board where a list of contributors is displayed, with, beside each name, a small symbol or design representing something she/he likes about her/himself. Otherwise, as Orlick says, children won't 'know how to help one another, to be sensitive to another's feelings or to compete in a friendly, fun-filled way, even when they want to.'

In Co-operative Games, everybody wins and nobody can lose. 'These games eliminate the fear of failure.'

THE VALUES OF CO-OPERATIVE GAMES

Terry Orlick says there are four essential components to a successful co-operative game: Co-operation, Acceptance, Involvement, Fun.

Co-operation is closely related to communication and trust. In practical terms, says Wingate : 'Trust is physical contact, eye contact and shared laughter. Trust unites people, banishes fear and is the best state of mind for working together.'

He adds that teachers should, therefore, always join in playing Co-operative Games. They will learn a lot more by doing them than just teaching them. I have certainly found this to be so. And on communication, Wingate says the beginning of co-operation depends on the child's and teacher's ability 'to listen' and 'to understand another person's idea'. Through Co-operative Games, children learn to share and empathise. They work together as a unit and each player is a necessary part of the action.

Feelings of acceptance are directly related to increased self-esteem. This is the opposite of rejection and feelings of failure resulting from losing in a competitive situation.

I have heard a teacher of older children describe an experiment on rejection. Some of his pupils volunteered to wear purple armbands (purple was chosen because it has no particular political associations) for a period of two weeks, to see what reactions they got, but were not to tell anyone why, except their partners, who acted as supporters, helping to defuse the situations which arose, when necessary. The armbands acted as a form of social segregation and the children had to manage some very difficult situations; teachers in the school even refusing to teach a purple-armband child unless they were told what the symbol meant. This had interesting implications for the study of racism and minority groups in general.

Involvement is directly related to a feeling of belonging. There are several inventive ways of choosing partners in Co-operative Games books. For a pairs game, eg Mirrors (*Game A3 page 16*), Orlick suggested playing music. When it stops, children find a partner and play the game. Each time the process is repeated they have to find a different partner. Giving each child a jaggedly-cut half of a birthday card picture is another way. Masheder suggests choosing someone of your own height, or birthday month, or someone who is wearing the same colour as you. The variations are endless. Fun. They are. But the only way to discover this is to try them yourself.

Two more essential components of Co-operative Games are mentioned in another book: affirming ourselves and conflict-resolving.

The **Friendly Classroom for a Small Planet**, which describes itself as a **Handbook on Creative Approaches to Living and Problem-Solving for Children**, believes that poor self-image is at the 'root of many conflicts in school today', because if people don't feel positive about themselves, then they are unlikely to feel positive about others, and this prevents them from understanding another's point of view. It says this is the basis for many put-downs. It suggests group affirmation exercises which encourage children to look for positive characteristics in each other. I have felt the atmosphere in the classroom change whenever I have tried these. People relax and smile and look kindly at each other. These exercises are life-affirming.

Brearly suggests that it is relatively easy for young children to learn to say 'I'm sorry', but this is by no means the same as understanding the hurt feelings of another child. Weybright says that the development of true co-operation must be 'grounded in direct experience close to children's own area of interest'. I have found drama and role-play with puppets to be very useful for this. As Avon's **Peace Education Booklet** says: 'In fact, Peace Education does not advocate appeasement.. It does reject the eager willingness to resolve all issues by force, and argues that in spite of past experience and sometimes overwhelming difficulties involved, every effort should be made to seek resolution of conflict in non-violent ways.'

And as **The Friendly Classroom** points out: 'When children are given a loving, supportive environment, they seem better able to meet in a creative and reconciling manner situations inside or outside the classroom.'

Finally,as Masheder says: 'Co-operation is the first principle of peaceful conflict-solving'. People should be treated with kindness and with humour. *Working Together - a handbook for co-opeartion* shows how to use the different strengths of each individual so that all feel included and valued. It is a rich collection of practical lessons to teach (or should I say absorb) moral values – moral values in the best and widest sense. ■

A note on managing the games in the lesson plans:

The happiest co-operation involving adults and children are when co-operation flows freely both ways between the age groups. Co-operation isn't just children co-operating with adults, but also adults co-operating with children. On the matter of safety and fairness one method is to encourage all the group to take responsibility for these. Another is to take turns in responsibility. Whichever you choose it helps to get class agreement first.

It is the spirit not the rules that matter. To state the obvious, which can be forgotten in the pressure of circumstances,if you insist that unwilling children play co-operative games, the mood will be reluctant submission rather than co-operation. However inconvenient it may be, not all children want to play group games, co-operative or otherwise. Rather than insisting, let them watch or do something else, if you want to maintain the spirit of the activity.

Draft constitution for a new local group

The object of the group shall be:

l . To play co-operative games with people of all ages and all abilities (fit, disabled)

2. To play co-operative games at social clubs, schools, colleges, festivals, play schemes, hospitals, homes for children and the disable, etc.

3. To arrange special events for co-operative games primarily for fun and enjoyment, encouraging the less experienced to take increasing responsibility for introducing, steering and controlling games, to maximise co-operation and sharing of responsibility

5. To promote care and respect for our natural environment, friendship and understanding for all people, regardless of age, ability, shape, race, sex, sexual orientation, gender, cultural background, social status, etc. Through fun games with all people with brief reflective discussion during or after some session, to consider the benefits, implementations and limitations of co-operative games, where there are no winners or losers.

John Barker for New Games UK (extract)

evaluation

In recognition of the importance of evaluation in any new teaching approach, Terry Orlick in The Co operative Games and Sports Book suggests some questions which could be asked of participants of co-operative games, in order to get some detailed information and input from them, the players.

To do so, the following open-ended sample questions can be used either as a questionnaire or in an interview. Select or adapt those questions that seem suitable for your particular needs and age group.

If you do not have the time to ask all the questions, use the shortened form – the questions marked ✔

When new rules are introduced:

1. What did you think of those rules? Did you like them?

2. How much fun was it to play using these new rules as compared with using the regular rules?

✔ 3. What was the best thing about the new rules?

✔ 4. What was the worst thing about the new rules?

✔ 5. What ch anges could we make to the new rules to make the game more fun?

6. Do you think you would want to play using these rules again? Once everyone was used to them?

When new games are introduced:

1. What did you think of the game? Did you like it?

2. Who won? Did you win or lose?

3. Did you help in reaching the goal of the game? If yes, how?

✔ 4. What did you like best about the game?

✔ 5. What did you dislike most (or hate) about the game?

✔ 6. Have you got any ideas on how to make it more fun? Or ways to make it better?

7. Would you like to play it again?

When a new games programme is nearing completion (for example, here a series of co-operative games lessons):

✔ 1. What did you think of the new games?

2. Did you like them?

3. What did you like best about the games?

4. What did you dislike most (or hate) about the games?

5. Did you usually feel happy or sad when playing the games?

✔ 6. Which of the new games did you like best? Why?

✔ 7. Which of the new games did you dislike most? Why?

8. Did you feel that you were helping one another in the new games?

9. Did you ever feel that you lost in the new games? If yes, (a) when? and (b) how often? If no, why not?

10. Do you ever feel that you lose in regular games? If yes, (a) when?and (b) how often? If no, why not?

✔ 11. Do you know any ways to make new games better?

12. Do you know any ways to make regular games better?

13. If you could play any games you wanted in gym class (at picnics,play days, etc), what kind of games would you play?

14. Would you have any special rules?

With the youngest game players, one simple means of finding out how you have succeeded is to use pictures, such as smiling and sad faces, to indicate feelings. Immediately after the game is over, the players simply make a mark under the face with the expression closest to their feelings. With infant children, we use three faces (happy, in-between, sad); with retarded groups, just two faces (happy, sad); older groups respond to a range of five faces.

ORDER FORM

PARACHUTE GAMES

A comprehensive collection of co-operative games played with a parachute for pre-school, primary and mixed aged groups. Introduces participants to the value of co-operation in a highly enjoyable and non-doctrinaire way.

SAYING NO TO VIOLENCE children and peace

Saying no to violence looks broadly at what 'violence' might mean, and suggests practical and positive ways for parents and teachers of young children to come to grips with this contentious and essentially complex issue.

Saying no to violence shows how, if we want a less violent and more peaceful world, we must develop a positive vision of that world. We need to provide our children with real hope that such a world is possible; and we need to give them confidence in their ability to contribute towards it.

From smacking a child to bombing Afghanistan, violence is condoned and legitimised as a means of getting one's way – never mind the cost or efficacy. *Saying no to violence* locates some of the influences which condition our values and our understanding of violence within the cultural, political and economic system. It encourages critical examination of how culture and society expose children to violence. It offers practical suggestions for activities (many designed for KS2) and related discussion/story-telling both at home and in the classroom. Additional stories and resources at www.learnpeace.org.uk.

WORKING TOGETHER - a handbook for co-operation

Working Together is for people who think that co-operation is one of the most fruitful ways to forestall, reduce or resolve harmful conflict.

It provides practical suggestions for developing skills in working together and is supplemented by more theoretical material for discussion. It will be of particular use to parents, teachers, youth workers and anyone working with young people.

Co-operation, it argues, can redirect or eliminate competitiveness and retributive rivalry; it transcends the levelling aspects of compromise; it precludes violence and war.

The contents of this handbook are underpinned by the conviction that co-operative principles applied personally and locally can inform attitudes in wider environments, and thus work towards choosing a world free from war.

Return to PPU 41b Brecknock Road London N7 0BT   no copies

name _____   Parachute games £4.50   _____

address _____   Saying no to violence £9.99   _____

_____   Working together £9.50 _____

_____

enclose cheque for £ _____ or debit my credit card no _____

expiry date _____

CO OPERATIVE PLAY BOOKLIST

Manuals
Brandes D & Phillips H. **Gamesters' Handbook No.1**. Hutchinson.
Brandes D & Phillips H. **Gamesters' Handbook No.2.** Hutchinson.
Dearling A & Armstrong H. **Youth Games Book**. IT Resources.
Dearling A & Armstrong H. **World Youth Games**. Russell House
Fleugelman A. **New Games Book**. New Games Foundation.
Fleugelman A. **New Games Book and More Games**. Sidgwick & Jackson.
Masheder M. **Let's Play Together**. Green Print.
Macmullan T, ed. **Winners All.** Pax Christi.
Orlick T. **Co-operative Sports and Games Book: Challenge Without Competition**. Pantheon.
Olsen S & Parker J. **Parachute Games**. Peace Pledge Union.

Ideas/Philosophy
Borba M & C. **Self-Esteem: a Classroom Affair**. Harper & Row. Vol.1. and Vol.2.
Comell J. **Sharing Nature with Children.** Exley Publications.
Fine N. & Macbeth F. **Fireworks: Creative approaches to conflict**. Youth Work Press
Fine N. & Macbeth F. **Playing with fire: training for creative use of con-flict**. Youth Work Press
Heathcote D. **Collected Writings on Education and Drama**. Hutchinson.
Heathcote D. **Drama in the Education of Teachers**. University of Newcastle Institute of Education.
Jane E. **Life Skills Training Manual**. Community Service Volunteers.
Jones K. **Simulations.** Kogan Page.
Judson S. **Manual of Nonviolence and Children**. New Society
Kreidler W. **Creative Conflict Resolution**. Scott Foreman & Co.
Prutzmann P, et al. **Friendly Classroom for a Small Planet.** New Society Publishers.
Weinstein M & Goldman J. **Playfair**. Impact Publishers.